LOUIS VUITTON

"ICONS"

© 2006 Assouline Publishing
601 West 26th Street, 18th floor
New York, NY 10001, USA
Tel.: 212 989 6810 Fax: 212 647 0005
www.assouline.com

ISBN: 2 84323 903 6
EAN: 9782843239037

Translation from the French by Ann Wilkinson and Elena Luoto

Color separation by Gravor (Switzerland)
Printed by Grafiche Milani (Italy)

STÉPHANE GERSCHEL

LOUIS VUITTON

"ICONS"

Preface by Marc Jacobs

ASSOULINE

I remember my first collection for Louis Vuitton. We wanted to play a sort of peek-a-boo by using the gray Trianon canvas chosen to cover suitcases in the very beginning by Louis Vuitton himself. We opted not to use the Monogram, in order to better celebrate it later. My next idea was the hollowed Monogram Vernis, in matching tones that allowed us the opportunity to introduce rather acidic colors. Little by little, the cult of the Monogram became a topic of fashion. I think that what we undertook afterwards with Stephen Sprouse was unconsciously inspired by Marcel Duchamp, with his mustache-painting on the Mona Lisa that became the provocative L. H. O. O. Q. That is, the Monogram graffiti tagging is actually a tribute in the form of a desecration. With Takashi Murakami, his 36 colors and his cherries, we entered a play universe so terribly contemporary that it penetrates our own. It takes a healthy dose of courage and boldness if you are to put the workings of a big business into question. But fashion is cyclical, agitated by a perpetual movement. Like many actors, I have an essentially instinctive approach. With the passing of each collection I am always struck by a singular constant—the models who walk the runway with a Vuitton bag are always seemingly so much more Vuitton than the ones who do not. This really is the essential aspect of it all, it is not up to an icon to declare itself as such. These bags, our icons, have not become this way by chance, but by a conspicuousness that has imposed itself with the passing of years. These icons represent, all, together and each separately, the quintessence of the Louis Vuitton style.

Marc Jacobs,
Paris, July 2006.

ICONS

it was at the end of the 19th and the beginning of the 20th centuries, with the Industrial Revolution, that sea and air transportation were really able to develop. Within these modern concepts grew another idea, that of voyaging with elegance and comfort. Despite the advent of mass transport, this revolutionary approach to traveling continued to become more and more popular.

Founded in 1854, the House of Louis Vuitton joined the esthetes on their incessant quest for accessories worthy of a well-styled migration. First by packing their effects and protecting them in practical, stackable trunks that would withstand all the possible hazards of their sometimes perilous peregrinations. Later, by designing lightweight and distinctive soft bags, which would themselves evolve into fine leather goods.

However, summarizing Louis Vuitton's history in such a way is not doing it true justice. The fact is, that in the course of the last two decades, the House has asserted itself as the incontestable emblem of modern luxury. It derives its strength, not only from its know-how and perfectionism, but also from a strategic vision, constantly revisiting a very specific universe— an alchemy of French elegance that has been Louis Vuitton's unfailing tenet since its creation.

Even if the Monogram has become its legendary signature, to assume that the success of the trunk-maker is simply due to the canvas that covers its work is inexcusably negligent. Indeed, in the course of the last 150 years, the brand has elevated its creations to cult objects, the precursors of a fashion that has become timeless. Eleven of these accessories have been selected for special attention. These are the Icons of Louis Vuitton.

the Wardrobe (1875), the archetype of the trunk, was part of a collection of hard-frame luggage whose quality of craftsmanship and obvious distinction were the foundation for Louis Vuitton's success. The Steamer Bag (1901), the forerunner of soft bags, could be rolled up and stashed inside the compartment of a trunk, becoming the ultimate back-up bag. The same just-in-case function was filled by the Keepall (1930), revered as the prototype of all weekend totes. The Speedy was born in 1930, but it was in the 1960s, when it was redesigned in new dimensions for Audrey Hepburn, that it captured the hearts of countless women with its characteristic cubic shape. The Noé bag, made in leather as early as 1932, served to transport five bottles of champagne (four in a circle and one top to bottom). This holdall was one of the first to be made in supple Monogram canvas in 1959 and has since become the darling of active women. The Alma, designed in 1934, distinguishes itself by its shape—a true model of Art Deco. Reinvented in 1992, it quickly became a recognizable symbol of Louis Vuitton. These three bags are the House bestsellers.

The story of the Lockit bag is rather peculiar, for after its creation in the fifties it was subsequently forgotten. Rediscovered in the archives of the Vuitton family home in Asnières (now a museum), the Lockit was reissued in 2006 with the mission of continuing the glamorous conquest begun by the Papillon, adopted by the model Twiggy in the sixties, and the Bucket, seen less often in paddocks than in the front rows of fashion shows. Two additional icons join the nine aforementioned: the Soft Briefcase, originally a cover for cashmere rugs, is now a must for people who want to leave their mark on the business world; and the Amazone, initially designed for tropical explorers to pack away their photographic effects while on expedition, which has since been seized by more urban tribes.

S ince its creation, Louis Vuitton has entwined its destiny with numerous contemporary artists. In 1874, Louis and his son Georges went to visit their photographer friend Nadar. In his studio, he was hosting a group of then-unknown painters: Renoir, Pissarro, Sisley, Cézanne, Degas, Berthe Morisot... During one of their visits, the Vuittons noticed a Monet painting that had just been entitled, *Impression, Sunrise.* Some days later, by the hand of journalist Louis Leroy, the term "Impressionism" was born.

This episode marked the beginning of Louis Vuitton's enduring interest in the world of art in all its forms. At a time when his clients were named Jean Patou, Jean-Jacques Guerlain, Mistinguett, Jeanne Lanvin, or Mademoiselle Chanel, Gaston-Louis Vuitton appealed to Jean Puiforcat and Jean Dunant to create his silver and lacquer works, and to participate in the landmark Exposition des Arts Décoratifs of 1925. At the Paris Salon d'Automne in 1934, René Herbst presented a project for the French steel industry bureau OTUA. He had designed a cabin for an ocean liner, in the middle of which sat a set of monogrammed trunks. In the 1980s, Sol LeWitt, Arman and then César designed silk squares for the House, inaugurating a series of limited editions signed by the designers; meanwhile, Jean Larivière photographed his first, almost subliminal advertisements. In 1996, Louis Vuitton celebrated the centennial of the Monogram canvas with a brilliant collection of objects created by seven stylists: Azzedine Alaïa, Manolo Blahnik, Romeo Gigli, Helmut Lang, Isaac Mizrahi, Sybilla, and Vivienne Westwood. Presaging the arrival of

Marc Jacobs as the head of fashion in 1997, this collection opened the door for other collaborations such as Stephen Sprouse's graffiti in 2000, or Takashi Murakami's mischievous cherry that played on the Monogram in 2005.

L oyal to this collaborative tradition, Louis Vuitton has teamed up with nine designers of eclectic backgrounds: Shigeru Ban, Sylvie Fleury, Zaha Hadid, Bruno Peinado, Andrée Putman, Ugo Rondinone, James Turrell, Tim White-Sobieski and Robert Wilson. Their works will be displayed at the Espace Louis Vuitton from September 15 to December 31 2006 before, as worthy heirs to the Vuitton spirit, they embark on a voyage around the world...

Louis Vuitton stores, meanwhile, described as modern-day temples, might encourage a form of idolatry far removed from the original sense of the word icon, stemming as it does from a pious or orthodox representation. But if some see a certain fanaticism in the passions that run wild on this subject, let us remain iconoclasts. Is it ironic to speak of icons in the context of a luxury brand? On this subject, let us cite the words of French philosopher Vladimir Jankélévitch: "Irony is a form of modesty that veils a secret behind a curtain of pleasantries. But it is even more serious than the truly serious."

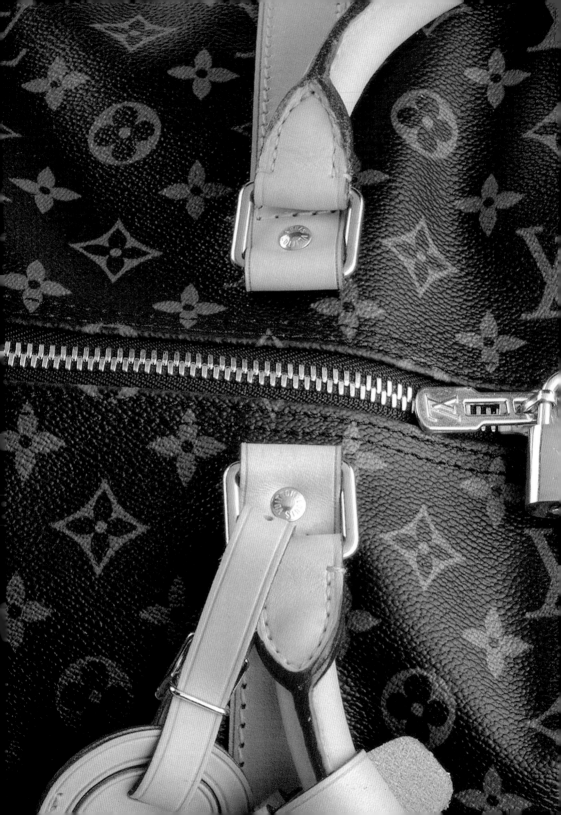

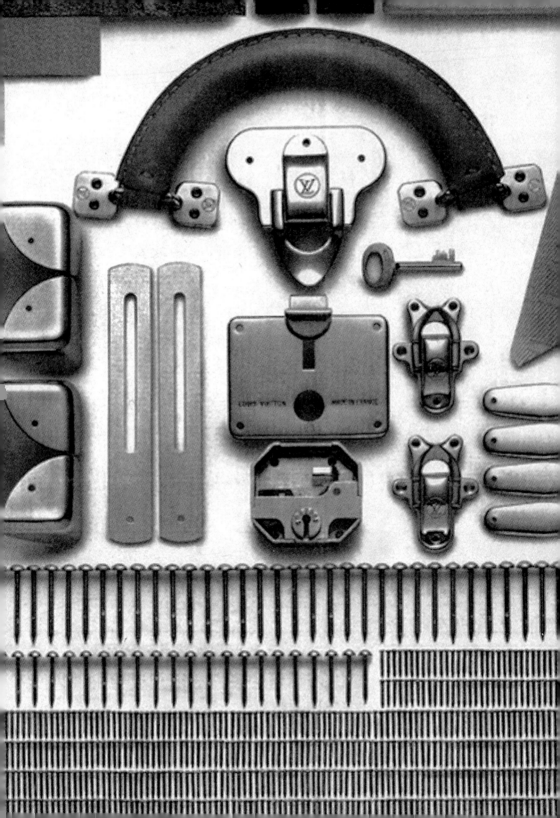

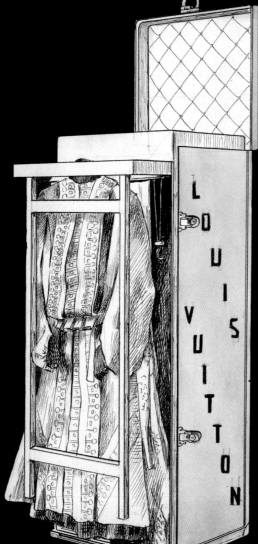

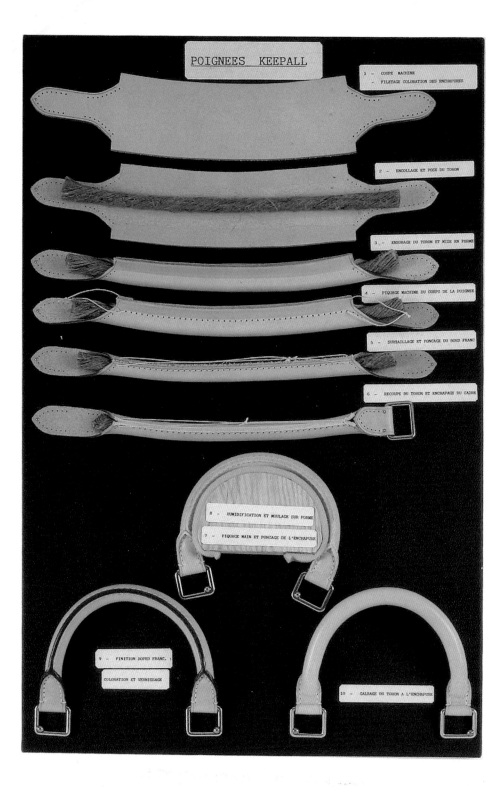

POIGNEES KEEPALL

1 - COUPE MACHINE
- FILETAGE COLORATION DES ENCHAPURES

2 - ENCOLLAGE ET POSE DU TORON

3 - ENROBAGE DU TORON ET MISE EN FORME

4 - PIQUAGE MACHINE DU CORPS DE LA POIGNEE

5 - SURTAILLAGE ET PONCAGE DU BORD FRANC

6 - RECOUPE DU TORON ET ENCHAPAGE DU CADRE

8 - HUMIDIFICATION ET MOULAGE SUR FORME

7 - PIQUAGE MAIN ET PONCAGE DE L'ENCHAPURE

9 - FINITION DUBORD FRANC.

COLORATION ET VERNISSAGE

10 - GALBAGE DU TORON A L'ENCHAPURE

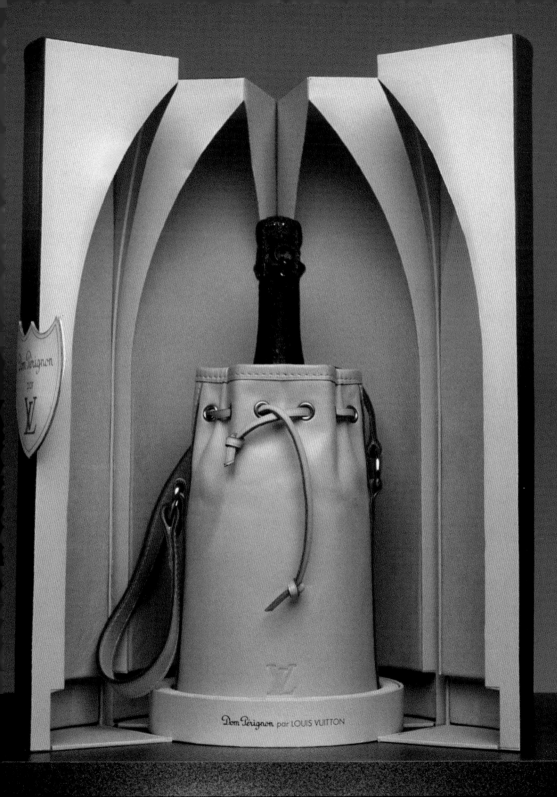

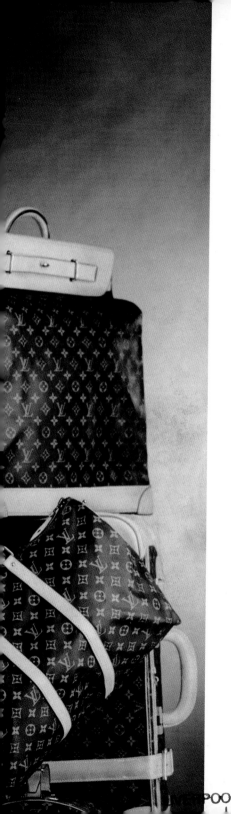

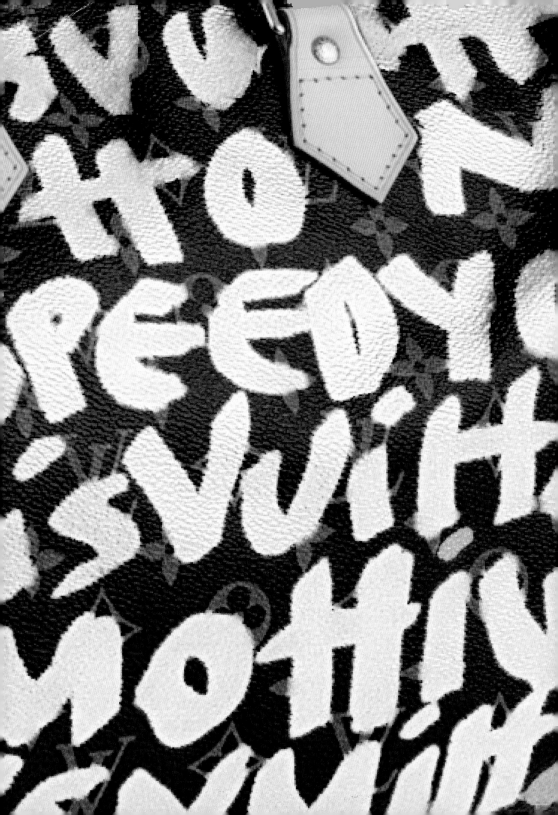

The Icons
by 9 Contemporary Designers

an artwork that reflects the made-up image of those looking at it feeds into the immemorial human need to decorate our reality. Fashion partakes in this same basic propensity to individuality. At the sometimes tenuous border between both creative disciplines, certain remarkable personalities have emerged—personalities we might describe, had the term not already been taken, as icons.

While Louis Vuitton was celebrating, not without a certain extravagance, the centenary of the Monogram canvas in 1996, a small revolution was underway. It was this movement that officially established the House as a leader in contemporary luxury—Louis Vuitton had entered the world of fashion.

Paris, Palais de Chaillot. In a tribal prelude to a celebration the like of which the world had never seen, Naomi Campbell prepared to share the spotlight with the Eiffel Tower. Accompanied by a giraffe, Campbell was dressed in leopard-skin—the same pattern that covered an Alma bag created by Azzedine Alaïa for the occasion. Also embodying fashion's avant-garde, Helmut Lang, Vivienne Westwood, Romeo Gigli, Manolo Blahnik, Isaac Mizrahi, and Sybilla each designed an object in tribute to the two legendary letters.

New York, 113 Spring Street. Far from Parisian pomp, Bernard Arnault visited Marc Jacobs' studio. Together, they finalized the contract that was to make the designer Artistic Director of Louis Vuitton. The announcement of Jacobs' arrival in 1997 offered an entirely new perspective on the flamboyant innovations of the previous year.

With each of his fashion shows, Marc Jacobs revisits the icons of the brand, inventing new ways to conjugate the Monogram, embossing it on brightly colored glazed leather and miniaturizing it on denim that is either colored or fringed. Stephen Sprouse was invited to "tag" the canvas in 2000, while in the spring of 2005 Takashi Murakami adorned it with a manga cherry. That same year, Louis Vuitton opened its new flagship House on the Champs-Elysées. Architects Peter Marino, Eric Carlson, and David McNulty combined their talents to concoct a spectacular 20,000 square foot space, the biggest to date. Confirming the trunk-maker's passion for art, three artists produced three original pieces for the House: with the help of fiber optic technology, Tim White-Sobieski created images for a 65-foot "traveling stair-case"; Olafur Eliasson invented a "senseless" elevator; and James Turrell composed one of his luminous sculptures.

Echoing the performance given at the Petit Palais to celebrate the opening of the House, the 7th floor Espace Louis Vuitton hosted its first exhibition with works by Vanessa Beecroft. Her photos of objectified live models offered a—to say the least—disturbing vision of the world of fashion.

In September 2006, this artistic space presents nine designers paying mischievous tribute to the Louis Vuitton icons by infusing them with their perceptions. The works of James Turrell, Andrée Putman, Sylvie Fleury, Bruno Peinado, Robert Wilson, Tim White-Sobieski, Ugo Rondinone, Shigeru Ban, and Zaha Hadid will then tour the world in a traveling exhibition.

The Wardrobe

by James Turrell

The son of a French aeronautical engineer who emigrated to the
United States, James Turrell has an unfailing passion for the
airplane built by his father. Today, Turrell flies the plane, which
is called the Harlow, himself. As its pilot he conquered the
American West by air, hunting out a site on which to establish
his studio. In 1974 he took up residence in an extinct vol-
cano—the Roden Crater—which was about to house a very dif-
ferent form of activity.

Having focused his work on the study of light, Turrell envisioned
a remarkable traveling trunk. When opened, it emits a brilliant
beam of 3-D light, which reacts to the surrounding radiance and
which the spectator, having unfolded the Wardrobe's built-in seat,
can observe at his leisure.

The Steamer Bag

by Andrée Putman

To the more customary description of her as "the great lady of design," Andrée Putman prefers the version coined by her friend, *Le Monde* journalist Michèle Champenois: "the vestal virgin of the immaculate conceptual." Having invented the modern hotel business by designing the first "boutique hotel" (the Morgans in New York, 1984), this multi-faceted discoverer has also reedited Jean-Michel Frank and Eileen Grey, and created the interior design for both the Air France Concorde and the offices of former French Minister of Culture Jack Lang.

A descendant of the Montgolfier brothers, the pioneers of aerostatic flight, Andrée Putman pays tribute to them by inviting the Steamer Bag to take off in a hot-air balloon. In a shower of Monograms, the bag reveals the black-and-white checkerboard beloved of the interior designer. Veiled in mist and with a sound ambiance suggesting an ocean liner preparing to cast off, the exhibit invites us to embark on "a journey with no destination, simply a journey."

A friend of Louis Vuitton, Andrée Putman also designed "Chemin Faisant," a limited-edition silk scarf, in 1994.

The Keepall

by Sylvie Fleury

Known for her protean artwork, Sylvie Fleury lives and works in Geneva. Her works consist of imagining, and then staging, the connection between art and society, fashion and its mechanisms. With impish humor and a keen sense of theatre, Sylvie Fleury artistically employs objects of daily life, especially those related to the idea of consumerism. Subtly provocative, her works conjure a truly original universe.

"I choose certain highly symbolic products from our consumer society, and reproduce them in the form of sculpture, generally in chrome-finish bronze. In this way, I give them a sort of shimmering immortality," explains Sylvie Fleury.

In 2000, she applied this process of readapting and "re-contextualizing" cult objects to the Louis Vuitton "Keepall," and reinvented the iconic bag as a ready-made in chrome-finish bronze—glorifying it, as it were, for keeps.

The Speedy

by Bruno Peinado

Born in 1970 in Montpellier, Bruno Peinado spent his childhood surrounded by artists, and inside the imaginations of intellectuals like Edouard Glissant. Today he lives in Brittany, when he is not traveling elsewhere. The artist, for whom "everything is subversive," does not believe in labels. Instead, he detects rhizome-like connections between each discipline he pursues. His references, whether Pop Art or Art Deco, are both numerous and spontaneous. What better way to characterize his process than by asking the man himself? "In the development of every artistic project there are ideas conjured from our unconscious as well as from our reality; this triggers reactions, some of which may be expected, and others necessarily unforeseen…"

For Louis Vuitton, Peinado takes on with gusto the legendary Speedy. From within this out-and-out city bag springs a virgin jungle inhabited by moving shadows. His creation consists of everything from aluminum sheets to numeric cut-outs. Alit with beams of strobe lighting, it is encircled by a halo that further adds to its mystery.

The Noé

by Robert Wilson

It is no doubt that with the impertinent "Einstein on the Beach," first staged at the Avignon Festival in 1976 and subsequently at New York's Metropolitan Opera, that Robert "Bob" Wilson made a name for himself. With his associate, the musician Philip Glass, he offered an insolent allegory of the genius of the modern world. Born in Texas, Wilson followed the teachings of painter George McNeil in Paris and worked with architect Paolo Solari in Arizona. He has lived in New York since the sixties, but escapes the city every summer to his Watermill Center in the Hamptons, where he brings together students and professionals from all creative disciplines.

In 2002, Robert Wilson conjured for Louis Vuitton a series of Christmas windows in psychedelic colors, whose spirit was echoed in a limited-edition collection of leather goods. On this occasion, he became the only person who has ever been authorized to modify the shape of the Monogram. The icon he has chosen, the Noé bag, is presented in an endless tunnel with two opposing sides, one black, one white, and takes on an almost ghostly appearance, which is accentuated by binary lighting effects recalling the dichotomy of all things.

TWO ís ONE

ROBERT WILSON

The Alma

by Tim White-Sobieski

First and foremost a New Yorker, and a graduate of Parsons School of Design, Tim White-Sobieski is a video artist whose works have been seen all around the world. He does not take his responsibility lightly: "Everywhere today there are screens imposing ever-moving, ever-changing information on us as passive passers-by, whether we want it or not. This proves the need for a new discipline, one that would take into account our individual capacity to detach ourselves. Even if information is perpetually scrolling before our eyes, and even if our brains absorb it all, we must still be able to determine which is worth retaining. Luckily, this subconscious process happens spontaneously for the vast majority of us."

Not without a certain sense of humor, Tim White-Sobieski created a film for Louis Vuitton that explores from within the intimate relationship between an Alma bag and its owner. The artist thus returns to the Champs-Elysées House, for which he previously designed the ambiance of the "traveling staircase."

The Lockit

by Ugo Rondinone

"My ambition is for Paris to creep into my composition, and for the bag, by some optical illusion, to appear as one of its monuments." A window opens onto the city of light and acquires, with the help of a color filter, enough unreality to become part of the work. The bag, hanging on the adjacent wall, takes its place in the landscape. Covered in bleached canvas, the Lockit also represents windows, symbols of universal correspondences between artificially compartmentalized worlds, expressed in the contrast of unrefined materials and objects of luxury.

Ugo Rondinone is Swiss. He divides his time between Zurich and New York, while simultaneously exhibiting in 2006 in Paris, New York, Aspen, London, Berlin, and Kraichtal-Unteröwisheim. His work draws on many diverse materials, from sophisticated video installations to non-manufactured outdoor elements like the branches of trees.

The Papillon

by Shigeru Ban

Japanese architect Shigeru Ban is a master of transforming materials normally considered temporary into permanent constructions. It is, he explains, all a matter of one's point of view: "During Japan's speculative bubble in the 1990s, buildings were built and then almost immediately pulled down by developers to make room for bigger ones. On the other hand, my paper church, constructed after the Kobe earthquake in 1995, was not meant to last more than a few years. However, it has recently been decided to move it to Taiwan, where it will become a permanent landmark." Cherishing, for his own work, structures made of paper tubes, Shigeru Ban has, for the "Icons" exhibition, covered them with Monogram canvas in an allusion to the cylindrical shape of the Papillon bag. As with his office atop the Pompidou Center in Paris, he has constructed a roof covering the top-floor balcony of the Champs-Elysées House.

The Bucket

by Zaha Hadid

Architect Zaha Hadid, winner of the 2004 Pritzker Prize for Architecture, is one of the most high-profile architects of our time. An advocate of "avant-garde architecture that transforms public space into civic space," her projects such as the Rosenthal Center for Contemporary Art in Cincinnati and the Phaeno Science Center in Wolfsburg, Germany, represent a portfolio that will soon include the Museum of Contemporary Art (MAXXI) in Rome and the Guangzhou Opera House in China. Hers is a sensual architectural language that reinterprets space and form. There is no doubt that Zaha Hadid will influence a generation of architects with her daring contrasts of supple forms and taut lines.

Zaha Hadid has created several versions of a futuristic Bucket bag—twisted and deformed, rounded and sharp—all clustered into the type of archipelago one would hope to discover on a journey to the stars.

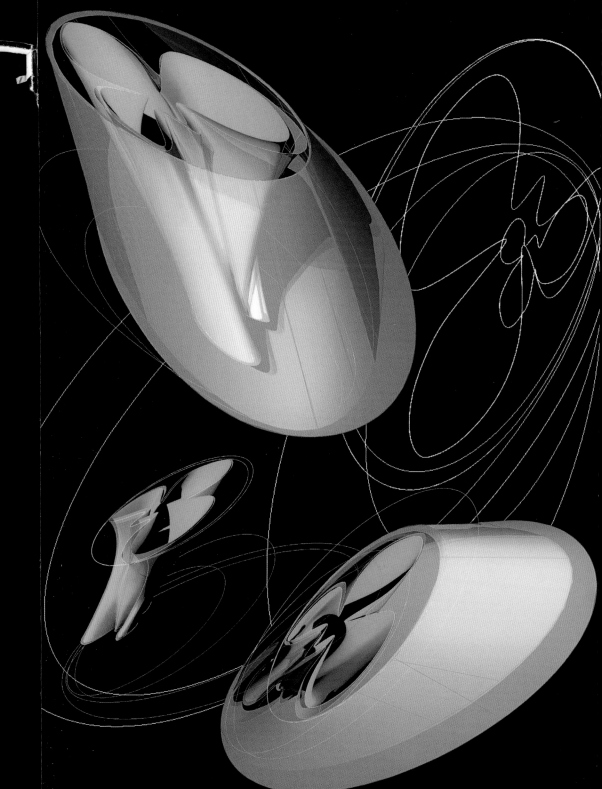

Icons

Wardrobe, 1875.

Steamer Bag, 1901.

Keepall, 1930.

Speedy, 1930.

Noé, 1932.

Alma, 1934.

Soft Briefcase, 1934.

Lockit, 1950.

Papillon, 1966.

Bucket, 1968.

Amazone, 1974.

75

LOUIS VUITTON

Detail of the zipper and gusset of the Alma Voyage in Monogram canvas. © Laurent Brémaud/LB Production.
Advertising insert that appeared in L'Illustration, May 24, 1930. © Louis Vuitton Archives.

Music trunk, or flycase, by Helmut Lang. Created for the centenary of the Monogram canvas in 1996, it was designed to hold the vinyl collection of a globe-trotting DJ. © Guzman.
Trunks in Damier canvas (1888) and gray Trianon canvas (1854). © Louis Vuitton Collection/Antoine Jarrier.

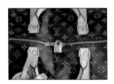

Detail of a Keepall in Monogram canvas. © Louis Vuitton.

Handles in natural leather and metal pieces in brass. © Louis Vuitton Japan. "The groom." © Jean Larivière.

Top: Keepall in cotton canvas with the emblem of Gaston-Louis Vuitton, around 1924. © Laurent Brémaud/LB Production. Bottom: Corporate advertising campaign "The Imaginary Journeys of Louis Vuitton", 1995. © Jean Larivière. Advertisement, around 1910. © Louis Vuitton Archives.

Four sizes of the Keepall. © Thierry Parant.

Advertising campaign "East Wind, West Wind", 1980. © Jean Larivière.

Original version of the Steamer Bag. © Alain Beulé.
Steamer Bag in Monogram canvas. © Pascal Louis.

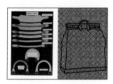

The Keepall's handle in various stages of manufacture. © Antoine Jarrier.
The outline of the Steamer Bag on an illustration of Monogram canvas. © Louis
Vuitton Archives/Assouline.

The Noé bag, created in 1932. It was originally designed for a champagne pro-
ducer who wanted a bag to hold five bottles. © Louis Vuitton Collection.
Special edition in natural cowhide for the Dom Pérignon 1990 vintage.
© Dom Pérignon Archives.

Fashion photograph published in Vogue and Paris Match in the 1960s. The Noé
bag in Monogram canvas appears alongside Cotteville, Bessac and Bisten hard-
frame luggage on the station platform reserved for the Mistral, the luxury train linking
Paris to the Riviera. © All rights reserved.

Alma bag in Damier canvas. © Laurent Brémaud/LB Production.
Lockit bag in Nomade leather. © Mitchell Feinberg.

Luggage in Monogram canvas, icons of the 1960s. © Télé Magazine, 1966. Poster for the exhibition celebrating Louis Vuitton's 150th anniversary at Galeries Lafayette. © Courtesy of Galeries Lafayette.

Alma Voyage bag in Monogram canvas. © Fabien Sarazin/Ôpos.

Orly Airport, Paris, October 14, 1969. Jane Fonda, with Roger Vadim, carrying a Speedy bag. © Rue des Archives.
Speedy bag in Monogram canvas. © Photographie: Thomas Lagrange/Installations Lumineuses: Thierry Dreyfus – production des installations: Eyesight.

Twiggy, the face of the sixties, with the Papillon bag. © Bert Stern/Condé Nast Publications.

Advertising campaign Fall/Winter 2002: Eva Herzigova with the Papillon bag. © Mert Alas and Marcus Piggott/Art Partner.

The biggest names in fashion have always been clients and friends of Louis Vuitton. Paul Poiret, Madeleine Vionnet, Jeanne Lanvin, Gabrielle Chanel, Christian Dior, Marcel Rochas, Jean Patou, Hubert de Givenchy, to mention but a few, feature on the client list. The world's most famous fashion editors, including Diana Vreeland and Anna Piaggi, have also contributed to the Louis Vuitton legend. © Ruben Toledo.

Monogram Graffiti canvas, created in 2000 in collaboration with New York artist Stephen Sprouse. © Antoine Jarrier.
Louis Vuitton fashion show, Spring/Summer 2001. © Dan and Corina Lecca.

Bucket bag in Monogram canvas. © Antoine Jarrier.
The Bucket bag in various materials. © Laurent Brémaud/LB Production. Cerises.
© 2004 Takashi Murakami/Kaikai Kiki co., ltd.

Speedy bag in Monogram Multicolore Franges. Monogram Multicolore est une création de Takashi Murakami pour Louis Vuitton. © Mitchell Feinberg.
Advertising campaign, 1998. Model: Diana Gartner/Viva. © Guzman.

Louis Vuitton Wardrobe in Monogram canvas. © Photographie: Thomas Lagrange/Installations Lumineuses: Thierry Dreyfus – production des installations: Eyesight.
The Louis Vuitton House on the Champs-Elysées, opened in 2005. © Jimmy Cohrssen.

p. 4: **Louis Vuitton Fashion show,** spring-summer 2003.
© Giovanni Giannoni/WWD. Sacs en toile Monogram Multicolore.
Monogram Multicolore est une création de Takashi Murakami pour Louis Vuitton.

The Icons by 9 contemporary Designers:
p. 57 : Collection Louis Vuitton 2006 © James Turrell.
p. 59 : Collection Louis Vuitton 2006 © Andrée Putman.
p. 61 : Collection Louis Vuitton © Sylvie Fleury/Photo Laziz Hamani/Assouline.
p. 63 : Collection Louis Vuitton 2006 © Bruno Peinado.
p. 65 : Collection Louis Vuitton 2006 © Robert Wilson.
p. 67 : Collection Louis Vuitton 2006 © Tim White-Sobieski.
p. 69 : Collection Louis Vuitton 2006 © Ugo Rondinone.
p. 71 : Collection Louis Vuitton 2006 © Shigeru Ban.
p. 73 : Collection Louis Vuitton 2006 © Zaha Hadid.

The author would especially like to thank Yves Carcelle and Rebecca, as well as Martine Assouline, for their renewed confidence and informed advice.
Thank you to Marc Jacobs for his kindly good humor and to Patrick-Louis Vuitton for his friendly reassurance regarding the veracity of our words.
Thank you to Marie-Sabine Leclercq and Eléonore de Boysson for their unfailing commitment to this project.
Thanks again to Antoine Jarrier, Nathalie Tollu, Marie-Ange Moulonguet, Frédéric Devenoge and Jun Fujiwara for their patience and daily assistance.
And finally thank you to the designers: Shigeru Ban, Sylvie Fleury, Zaha Hadid, Bruno Peinado, Andrée Putman, Ugo Rondinone, James Turrell, Tim White-Sobieski, and Robert Wilson, for their kindness and availability.

The editor would especially like to thank Laurent Brémaud (LB Productions), Grand Master Flash, the Guzmans, Jean Larivière and Fatima Hamlil, Thierry Parant, Alain Beulé, Madame Debever (Dom Pérignon Archives), Patrick Skacha and Mitchell Feinberg, Inji Massoteau (Agence Opos), Stéphanie Grall (Galeries Lafayette), Catherine Terk (Rue des Archives), Marcelle Wong (Creative Artists Agency), Marie-José Lauer (Agence BETC), Thea Martin (PFD), Bert Stern, Candice Marks (Art Partner), Pascale Duchemin (City Models), Ruben Toledo, Dan and Corina Lecca, Chantal Fagnou (Viva), Jimmy Cohrssen and Carrie Provenzano (WWD), Leigh Montville (Condé Nast Publications).